DATE DUE

95.41.57

FROM MAP TO MUSEUM
Uncovering Mysteries of the Past

By Joan Anderson, Photographs by George Ancona

Introduction by Dr. David Hurst Thomas
Curator of Anthropology, American Museum of Natural History

Morrow Junior Books, New York

Acknowledgments

We gratefully acknowledge Dr. David Hurst Thomas and his
team of archaeologists, who helped us understand the process
of archaeology as they probed the mission on St. Catherines.
Particularly hospitable were Lorann Pendleton Thomas and
Royce Hayes, Superintendent of St. Catherines Island. Back
at the museum, we appreciated the help of Debra Peter,
Melanie LeMaistre, Margo Dembo, Judith Levinson, Ralph
Bauer, and Belinda Kaye. Telephone interviews with the
following people helped fill in the gaps of information not
available to us on site: Rosa Lowenger, Project Conservator;
Dennis O'Brien, Project Artist; and Amy Bushnell,
Historian.

Thank you all.   Joan Anderson   George Ancona

PHOTO CREDITS   American Museum of Natural History, pp. 19, 23, 25, 27, 29,
30, 32–33, 39 (both); P. K. Yonge Library of Florida History, University of Florida,
p. 35; University of North Carolina Press, p. 8. Permission is gratefully acknowledged.

Printed in the United States of America.
1 2 3 4 5 6 7 8 9 10
Library of Congress Cataloging-in-Publication Data
Anderson, Joan.
    From map to museum.
    Includes index.
    Summary: Describes an archaeological dig off the coast of Georgia, the methods used
to uncover artifacts there, and what was learned about a mission run there by the
Spanish for the Guale Indians.
    1. Guale Indians—Missions—Juvenile literature. 2. Guale Indians—
Antiquities—Juvenile literature. 3. Saint Catherines Island (Ga.)—Antiquities—
Juvenile literature. 4. Missions—Georgia—Saint Catherines Island—Juvenile
literature. 5. Indians of North America—Georgia—Saint Catherines Island—
Missions—Juvenile literature. 6. Indians of North America—Georgia—Saint
Catherines Island—Antiquities—Juvenile literature. 7. Archaeology—
Methodology—Juvenile literature. 8. Georgia—Antiquities—Juvenile literature.
[1. Guale Indians—Antiquities. 2. Indians of North America—Georgia—Antiquities.
3. Saint Catherines Island (Ga.)—Antiquities. 4. Georgia—Antiquities.
5. Archaeology—Methodology]
I. Ancona, George, ill.   II. Title.
E99.G82A54   1988   975.8'733   87-31307
ISBN 0-688-06914-2
ISBN 0-688-06915-0 (lib. bdg.)
Book design by George Ancona

To Martha Masterson—J.A.

To Ira Herrick—G.A.

Contents

Introduction

For the last fifteen years, I've worked as an archaeologist for the American Museum of Natural History, in New York City. My museum owns more than thirty-six million artifacts and scientific specimens. No institution anywhere has more dinosaurs, birds, spiders, fossil mammals, or whale skeletons. The American Museum is the largest natural history museum in the world.

If you're like most people, you'll start a visit to the American Museum with the dinosaurs. When you tear your eyes off the toothy grin of a twenty-foot *Tyrannosaurus,* you can stare down the throat of a fifty-foot crocodile, track a set of dinosaur footprints, or inspect four nests of dinosaur eggs. Across the room is a prehistoric mummy, a duck-billed dinosaur with skin still stretched over the bones, complete down to the webbed feet.

You'll probably also take in the cavelike Hall of Minerals and Gems, where you can touch a dozen meteorites from outer space, slide down an eight-foot slab of jade, and gaze at priceless gems such as the breathtaking Star of India. The forty massive exhibition halls display thousands of such curiosities. To most people, these world-famous exhibition galleries *are* the American Museum.

But there's more to a museum than just the skeletons, precious stones, and artifacts. Every object has a story to tell.

Remember the dinosaur eggs? What a tale they told. In 1922, the American Museum of Natural History sent an expedition to the Gobi Desert of Outer Mongolia. They were looking for the "missing link," but they found dinosaur eggs instead.

Once the word leaked out, the eggs of *Protoceratops* became worldwide celebrities. Some people even speculated that the eggs could be incubated and hatched! Imagine watching a baby dinosaur hoist itself out of an egg—all right here in our museum laboratories.

The dinosaur eggs had, of course, turned to stone (fossilized) one hundred million years or so ago, so no baby dinosaurs are hopping through the museum corridors. But the fossil eggs remain a fabulous scientific discovery. Up to that time, paleontologists could only guess how little dinosaurs came to be. Were they born, hatched, spawned, or what? Now scientists can not only inspect unhatched eggs, but also study the fossil skeletons of several embryos and newborns.

More than 2.6 million people view such specimens at the American

Museum each year. But how many realize that a live, working scientist might be tucked away behind their favorite exhibit? Each day some of the world's most famous -ologists—paleontologists, anthropologists, ichthyologists, entomologists, and archaeologists—hurry through these halls on their way to study new finds and make new discoveries.

I'm an archaeologist and I may have dug up some of the artifacts you see in the museum cases. In this book, Joan Anderson offers you the chance to tag along on a real archaeological expedition. Why not sign up as a member of my team?

Together we'll slog through the swamps of the Sea Islands, searching for a lost Spanish mission. You'll find out how we know where to dig. (Did you know that we now use space-age technology to learn about our past?) You can help excavate the ruins of Mission Santa Catalina, peering over my shoulder as we dig up artifacts buried centuries ago. We'll take our finds to my museum laboratory, where you'll meet conservators, who stabilize and preserve them. And as we study the artifacts, you will uncover clues about America's unknown, remote past.

The objective of a museum is to learn, and then pass this new knowledge on to others. You'll walk through our labs and studios, where we'll work with artists and designers to create a new exhibit showing off our discoveries.

When you get back from this "dig," you'll be able to pick out a favorite artifact in a museum and make it "yours." The label may tell you how old it is and where it came from. But if you really concentrate, maybe that artifact will speak to you directly. Think about the people who used it. Was it difficult to make? Where did the raw materials come from? Was it valuable? Was the artifact broken and deliberately discarded? Or was it lost accidentally?

In these pages, you'll see where artifacts came from, and how they end up in a museum. As you transport yourself across space and through time, try to sense, feel, taste, and touch the past. Museum artifacts form our bridge to people and cultures that have vanished. *From Map to Museum* shows how that bridge was built.

Dr. David Hurst Thomas
CURATOR OF ANTHROPOLOGY
AMERICAN MUSEUM OF NATURAL HISTORY,
NEW YORK

The little boy holds his father's hand tightly and gazes into the display case. As crowds of museum visitors bustle by, the man reads aloud from the sign that hangs nearby and describes the artifacts inside the case. There is a beautiful cross that once belonged to an Indian boy who lived four hundred years ago. It is an exciting moment for father and son. They are Native Americans. Their ancestors came from the southeastern part of the United States, like the Guale Indians who are the subject of this museum exhibit. Until now there has been little information about these tribes.

Apart from the crowds a bearded man stands unobtrusively in one corner of the gallery. He watches with obvious delight as the people move from one display case to another. He is Dr. David Hurst Thomas, Curator for the American Museum of Natural History in New York City. An archaeologist and anthropologist, he is the man responsible for finding these priceless treasures and uncovering the lost mission on St. Catherines Island off the coast of Georgia.

As he gazes at the steady stream of visitors filing past him, he is confronted by a group of journalists eager to report the story of this newest discovery.

"Where did this all begin?" one reporter asks him. "I mean how did these things get here?"

Leaning lightly against a nearby display case, Dr. Thomas searches his mind for the best answer. "Well," he begins, "the best way to explain an archaeological exploration is to compare it to a scavenger hunt. In a scavenger hunt the players are given a map and it's up to them to figure out landmarks and clues. Archaeologists, if they're lucky, have a map or two as well as historical data that provide clues to where the 'treasure' or the lost site may be."

Moving toward a series of maps displayed on one of the exhibition hall walls, he points to a complicated-looking one, complete with ancient sailing ships and old-fashioned designs.

"It all began about fifteen years ago," he explains. "We started off with a couple of hunches and this map here. . . ."

Dr. Thomas's only historical map summarizes everything that he knew about the location of the Spanish mission system in the Southeast. At first glance it would appear that much was known. However, a closer look shows just how vague this map is—it does not indicate where the mission on St. Catherines might have been.

1. *How the Hunt Began*

David Thomas was sitting in his fifth-floor office, hidden away from the thousands of museum visitors walking the halls beneath him. He was putting the finishing touches on his latest manuscript when the phone rang. The caller was one of the museum's administrators.

"I've just had a call from a fellow down in Georgia," the man said rather matter-of-factly. "Seems there's an island called St. Catherines that might have some real archaeological possibilities."

"Such as?" Dr. Thomas queried, perking up ever so slightly.

"Well, he wasn't very specific. He just said that there has recently been renewed interest in the Spanish missions of the Southeast and that St. Catherines was thought to have been one of the most important."

"Sounds interesting," David answered. "Anything else?"

"They'd like someone from here to come down and see what he thinks. Because of your expertise, I thought you'd be the perfect candidate."

"Are you giving me the go-ahead to run off and do the field study?" David asked jokingly. "Because if you are, I'd be delighted." For David, being an archaeologist is like being a detective. The very mention of a new challenge or mystery to be solved was fuel enough for his investigative fires.

"Supposedly the island was once populated by Guale Indians whom the Spanish were hoping to convert," the man continued.

David's mind was racing. With so many Spanish missions along the West Coast, David, a Californian, had always been possessed with mission mania. He was intrigued with the possibility of investigating Spanish missions on the East Coast. So little was known of these missions.

"Well then, I'll tell them you'll be down in a couple of weeks," David's caller said. "It shouldn't take you longer than that to go over the material we have on file about the area."

And with that, he hung up.

David Thomas sat back in his chair to catch his breath. He could hardly believe what had just taken place. Usually explorers such as David had to struggle to get time off and hunt for funding before they could begin a project. This seemed almost too easy!

He shook his head, deciding not to question the opportunity any further, and began instead to scan his private library for relevant information. He was hoping to find a description of what missions in the Southeast might have looked like. He also sought historical accounts written by people who had lived or visited the island hundreds of years ago.

As he went through the available research, he was interested to learn that archaeologists from the University of Georgia had conducted previous searches on St. Catherines. Their field notes would be most helpful at the outset.

Further search of the archives brought forth notes written by a Spanish priest in the seventeenth century describing coastal Georgia and its waterways. There was also a list compiled by a Spanish bishop that identified some twenty-seven missions in the southeastern part of North America, and an account of a Spanish governor's visit to St. Catherines Island in 1675.

"This kind of evidence," thought David, "suggests that the Spanish considered the place rather important."

He was encouraged by this initial evidence, but as an archaeologist, he knew that the real story of what had happened on St. Catherines would only come from the ground itself.

2. *Going with the Hunch*

Several weeks later Dr. Thomas was ready to depart for St. Catherines. He carried with him three pieces of evidence. A map was found that had been drawn up in the 1930s by John Tate Lanning, a historian who studied the Spanish mission system and was able to indicate the location of each mission along the Georgian coast. He also had a journal entry from an early seventeenth-century Spanish governor named Ybarra describing how he and his entourage walked a half mile inland after disembarking from their vessel. Probably such a vessel would have been looking

for a calm harbor or inlet in which to moor. David, using his modern-day map, would be investigating the decent-sized waterways and harbors, such as Chapala Creek, that might accommodate such a vessel.

David headed to the coast of Georgia, traveled thirty miles south of Savannah, boarded a small power boat, and headed five miles out into the Atlantic Ocean.

He stared ahead as the craft wound through the marshland that was typical of southern waters, anxious for his first glimpse of the island. Eventually a hump of land appeared on the horizon. As the boat brought him closer, the mound was transformed into a lush tropical island. Palm trees swayed in the breeze, and Spanish moss dangled from the limbs of oaks.

David's heart pounded with excitement as he scanned the coastline and the boat approached the island's crude wooden dock.

He had two major objectives: to determine if St. Catherines, with its sandy soil and eroded beaches, lent itself to an archaeological dig, and to see if he could find any surface clues as to where a mission might have once existed. Although several field teams from the University of Georgia found considerable Spanish material several years prior to David's visit, none of their minor excavations yielded any structural evidence of a mission.

Dr. Thomas's first job was to borrow the island's power boat and circle St. Catherines in order to grasp its size and get a general overview. He was looking for those inlets and natural harbors that Governor Ybarra had described.

Then, using his present-day map, he was going to use the island's jeep and travel to the areas that previous explorers had mentioned as possible locations for the lost mission.

Finally, he intended to traverse the island, looking for clues, asking himself questions, attempting to arrive at answers, and always, always recording his thoughts and initial conclusions on his tape recorder.

Archaeologists know that wherever they walk, most likely many others had walked years before them. There is almost a reverence as they travel about trying to imagine who had inhabited the area and how they might have lived. "What we know is invisible," Dr. Thomas is fond of saying. "The evidence lies in the ground."

The week went by quickly. He didn't find any substantial surface evidence and deduced from the few historical accounts available to him at this point, that the mission buildings had probably been constructed of perishable materials such as wood, thatch, and mud. One mighty ocean storm could easily have blown the structures away or washed them out to sea—if the mission was located near a shoreline. But the hardened mud floors should be somewhere under the sandy soil, and David was excited at the prospect of uncovering them.

David gave St. Catherines a high score as a good place for a dig. Since no one had lived here for years, the land was relatively undisturbed. Furthermore, it remained that way because the general public was not allowed access.

As the boat pulled away from the dock and he headed back home, David watched St. Catherines disappear on the horizon. He was intrigued by the island and what lay beneath its surface. He felt that it held many secrets, and he was gratified that he was going to have the opportunity to uncover them.

3. *Scratching the Surface*

While Dr. Thomas was doing his on-site evaluations, his staff at the museum continued their search for historical information. Previous explorers had found Spanish pottery from the seventeenth century near Chapala Creek, as well as a few nails of the type that Spaniards once used to build their Georgian missions.

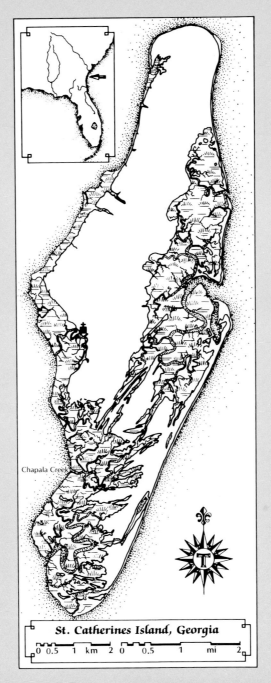

Chapala Creek

St. Catherines Island, Georgia

0 0.5 1 km 2   0 0.5 1 mi 2

Dr. Thomas's modern-day map. Maps such as this helped lead him to possible settlement areas.

19

Nevertheless, with so little historical information and surface evidence, a good scientist like David Thomas knew that there weren't enough clues to suggest that the mission was in one specific area. Field crews would have to comb the entire ten-mile-long island—being very careful in the spots where objects had been found—before excavation could begin in any one location.

And finding the site wasn't going to be easy: The island was the size of Manhattan in New York City, and this mission was probably no larger than two-and-one-half football fields. Dr. Thomas realized that he would have to organize several crews and spend many years in the search.

The first field crew of eleven people was chosen, and several months after David's initial visit they departed for St. Catherines Island to begin the arduous task of a randomized systematic survey—a process somewhat like combing the beach for lost jewelry.

Wearing special clothes to protect them from mosquitoes, ticks, and snakes, they walked eleven abreast, with several feet in between them. They traversed the island from east to west, encountering uncomfortable brush, fallen trees, and alligator-infested swamps as they walked. They were searching for surface clues of past life and small mounds of earth in an otherwise flat area.

As structures are built and then fall down and decay, new buildings arise atop the old, and the ground gradually builds up, forming a mound. Mounds also form where people discard their rubbish over the years.

In the case of St. Catherines, the archaeologists were looking for mounds that consisted of clusters of oyster and clam shells. Although shells were readily visible on the surface, the team was equally interested in finding subsurface shell deposits. Since the Indians and settlers would probably have eaten these coastal water shellfish, such "rubbish piles" might indicate that human habitations were nearby.

After three years and eleven separate visits, they eventually discovered 135 archaeological sites. And by probing the ground at several of them, it became more and more evident from the cultural evidence they found that the western part of the island was the place that deserved the most investigation.

4. *Charting the Clues*

Until now David and his crews depended, for the most part, on a few old maps and notes to guide them toward the mission site. But with the evidence mounting from the randomized survey that the area to concentrate on would be the western part of St. Catherines, the project artist now began to draw up maps and charts to record and control the next steps of the exploration.

First the artist drew a map showing the results of the survey. His map indicated where the field teams had searched and where they had found the most Spanish ceramics. Those places were circled and the map then showed that Spanish evidence was concentrated in the western part of the island, particularly near Chapala Creek.

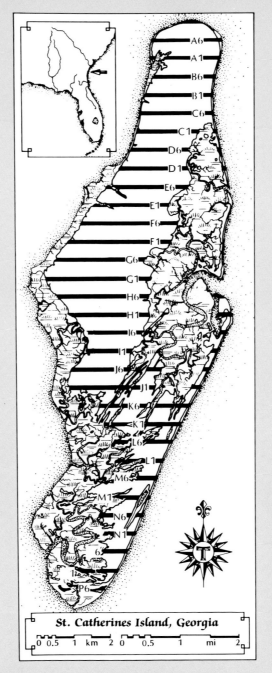

St. Catherines Island, Georgia

0   0.5   1 km 2   0   0.5   1   mi   2

Once the randomized systematic survey was complete, the project artist drew a map showing precisely where the crew walked and the specific area they covered. As Spanish material was found, its location would be indicated. Most of the evidence was found on the western side of the island.

So another map was drawn of the area near the creek. The ground near the creek had been roped off and carefully defined. A grid system was imposed and on the newly created map, the area began to resemble a checkerboard. Each square was labeled a quad. Each quad was given a number. As the archaeologists began looking for evidence in the area, they recorded the specific quad from which their findings came. In so doing, they hoped they could find the mission.

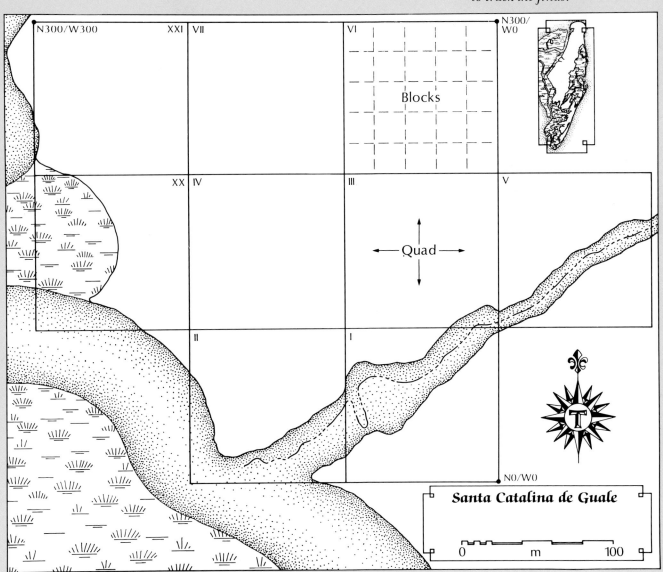

N300/W300 XXI VII VI N300/W0

Blocks

XX IV III V

Quad

II I

N0/W0

Santa Catalina de Guale

0   m   100

With the help of a digging machine called a power auger, another field crew was able to unearth great amounts of reddish clay. As the power auger thrust deep into the soil, crew members inspected the chunks of matter that were shooting out. They began to realize that it was daub, a material known to have been used by the Indians to construct buildings.

They dug 615 pits. Shards, bone fragments, and pieces of shells were evaluated on the spot, and their original location and density were plotted on yet another map.

David could see that shard density varied considerably but was especially high in certain quads, particularly number four. More than one third of all the shards of Spanish origin had been found there. It was becoming more and more obvious that they were getting close to something.

"The less we can destroy," Dr. Thomas told his crew, "the better. We'd best stop tampering with the area, however tempting it might be right now." David knew that archaeological sites are nonrenewable resources. Once a shovel goes into the ground things underneath can never be the same.

Modern technology permits an archaeologist to dig less and find more. Dr. Thomas was ready to call in a magnetometer team equipped with a machine that

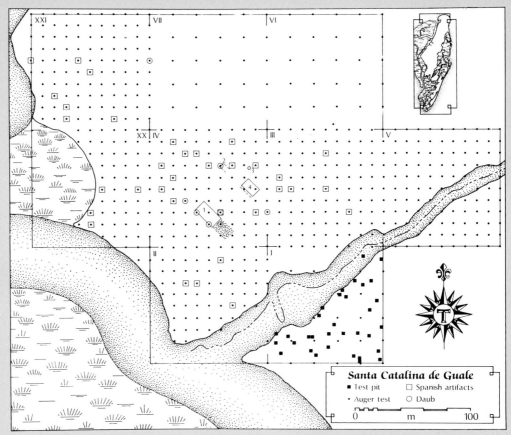

Santa Catalina de Guale

■ Test pit   □ Spanish artifacts
• Auger test   ○ Daub

0   m   100

This map indicates all the places where the excavators dug or penetrated with the power auger. From this chart they could see the distribution of mission material, much of which appeared to be located in Quad IV. (The locations of Spanish period structures that are now known have been added for reference.)

scans the ground and produces a computer printout indicating foreign substances that are beneath the surface.

Such a team from the University of Texas arrived. After traversing the area near Chapala Creek with their magnetometer, they were able to confirm everyone's suspicions. "If we were y'all, we'd dig in three places: right here," the head of the team said, pointing to the ground beneath him, "over yonder, and especially right here."

With only a few days left to work before he had to return to the museum, David Thomas and his crew quickly dug a few test pits in those three areas. Finally, the earth might yield the rewards the searchers had been hoping for!

The "over yonder" area contained a huge concentration of burnt daub, an unfired clay floor, charcoal, a single nail, and some Spanish ceramics.

In the "right here" section the excavators found a small mound that contained more daub, deer bones, iron spikes, fragments of olive jars, and other ceramics.

The "especially right here" area surrendered a Spanish barrel well. This is always an exciting find for an archaeologist, because wells, when excavated, generally contain nicely preserved artifacts.

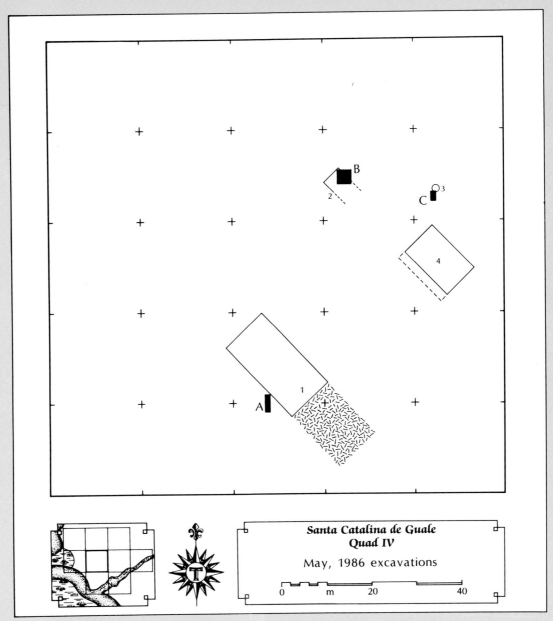

The solid-colored boxes on this map show where the magnetometer indicated foreign materials lay beneath the surface. "Over yonder" is A; "right here" is B; and "especially right here" is C.

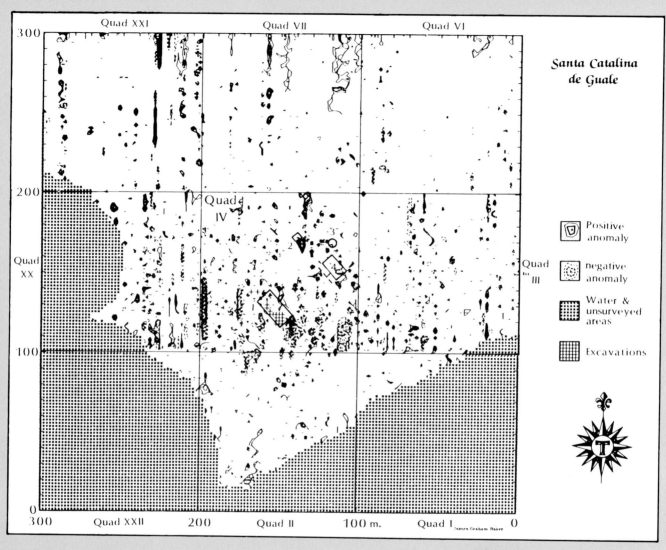

Quad XXI   Quad VII   Quad VI

Santa Catalina
de Guale

Quad
IV

Quad
XX

Quad
III

Positive
anomaly

negative
anomaly

Water &
unsurveyed
areas

Excavations

Quad XXII   200   Quad II   100 m.   Quad I

James Graham Baker

*This actual printout from the
magnetometer confirmed that
the Quad IV area had a high
concentration of foreign objects.*

Electronic technology more than paid off for David and his field teams. He soon received computer print-out maps specifying more clearly just where the foreign objects beneath the ground were located.

But for now, he felt sure enough to have Quad IV cleared of the scrub and trees that engulfed it.

With the probabilities narrowed, Dr. Thomas's research objective now shifted from locating the site to the more exciting work of uncovering artifacts. The team could now begin to dig up the long sought-after treasures; a new phase of discovery had begun!

5. *Breaking Ground*

Eight years had passed since the first exploratory trip and now, after matching physical clues to historical facts, the real action was about to take place.

Soil resistivity experts had ascertained the presence of metal, daub, and other foreign substances in the ground by placing electrodes in the soil and passing an electrical current between them. The current is interrupted by any subsurface object it encounters.

Aerial photographs revealed lines in the ground that indicated the presence of structures below the surface.

This aerial photograph was taken after several excavation trips. Mission structures are clearly visible in it. Earlier aerial photographs revealed marks on the ground indicating areas where structures might have existed.

With this additional evidence, the first excavation crew dug trenches in Quad IV, attempting to locate the boundaries of the supposed mission walls.

Information was continually being fed to the field teams by historians from regional universities as well as by the staff back at the museum. One important discovery was a description of what Spanish missions were supposed to look like by ordinance of the King of Spain. Since the king wanted all the missions to look alike, his decree provided David and his crew with their first model of the "shape" of things to come. A rare map of another mission in the southeastern part of North America was also found which outlined a typical period mission compound.

As Dr. Thomas searched through the rubble for walls he hoped he might find, he was constantly making pictures in his head about what the mission might have looked like.

"I'm not digging daub," he would say to himself. "I'm digging up walls!"

Eventually three separate structures became distinguishable: a mission church, the friars' living quarters, and the kitchen.

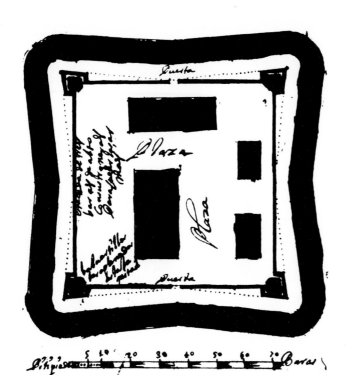

This seventeenth-century map provided Dr. Thomas with a model of southeastern missions. It was helpful in suggesting the dimensions of the mission on St. Catherines.

Once the structures were clearly defined, each area within Quad IV was roped off and the real excavation work began. The site was divided into squares called units until it looked like a piece of graph paper. Each excavator worked in an individually marked unit, scraping away soil. Every six to eleven inches, the soil was labeled. These marked-off layers are called zones.

Surprises abound in archaeology; at any moment an important clue to the past might emerge. And because of the magnetometer's printout, these diggers were sure that archaeological treasures indeed lay beneath the surface. Unlike their early predecessors, who must have felt as though they were searching for a needle that *might* be in a haystack, these excavators not only knew that there definitely were many "needles" to be found but also where they should look for them.

6. *Touching Treasures*

A typical day began before dawn. Sleepy workers boarded a van that took them from their living quarters through the early morning mist to the excavation site. Observing them unloading their equipment and beginning to "dig in," someone could have mistaken them for construction workers about to lay a foundation for a new home. Instead of building up, however, these builders of the past were digging down.

Using trowels, the excavators went over every inch of their unit, not wanting to miss a thing. Every bit of soil that was removed from a unit was put into a bucket and screened, or sifted, to make sure that no secret from the ground would be lost.

Screeners searched through the soil and found tiny beads, pieces of glass, fish vertebrae, and shards. They placed all their finds in plastic bags, categorized them, and put similar types of objects in larger paper bags.

The diggers were never without their clipboards because they constantly recorded notes. Whenever they found something, they marked the exact spot from which it was removed on their note pads before digging for more. This paper work is essential because, as Dr. Thomas explained, "Once we start digging, we are demolishing what is there, removing all the clues. It is only from the paper work, the copious notes, and the drawings that we are able to reconstruct the building and the answers we were searching for in the first place."

As the sun beat down on the busy workers, nothing was heard but the sound of the engines from the screening machine. The detailed work taking place required the utmost concentration. Everyone moved steadily—not too quickly, not too slowly, keeping on schedule but not at the expense of making mistakes.

The project artist continued to supply maps of the changing area. Moving from unit to unit, he recorded the look of the site as it varied from day to day. He drew pictures of the contents of trash pits, and, lying on his side in trenches, he recorded the various soil layers. He also photographed and drew the features as they were uncovered. A feature is an object that cannot or should not be removed from the site, such as a post or a large embedded object.

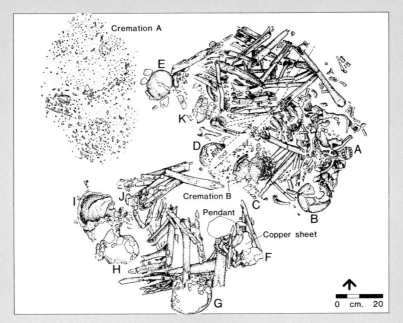

In the image: Cremation A, E, K, D, A, Cremation B, C, Pendant, Copper sheet, B, F, I, J, H, G

0   cm.   20

Burial mounds discovered by previous teams indicated the presence of a prehistoric Indian civilization on St. Catherines. The drawing shows what was exposed as the mound was excavated.

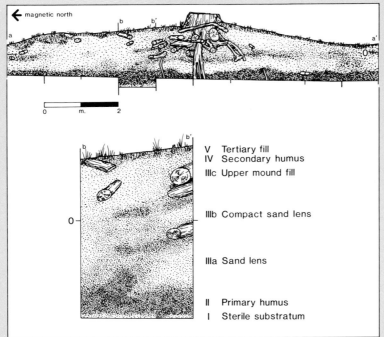

magnetic north

0   m.   2

V	Tertiary fill
IV	Secondary humus
IIIc	Upper mound fill
IIIb	Compact sand lens
IIIa	Sand lens
II	Primary humus
I	Sterile substratum

This is an artist's rendering of a mound and how it appeared as the various layers of earth were excavated.

39

By midmorning, artifacts began to appear and the silence was broken with comments: "Wow," one digger said to another, as he inspected a spot where a post had probably been dug. "Neat," another remarked when she discovered where the mission's oven must have stood. "David, I think I've found a medal," a third excavator announced excitedly. As everyone gathered around, Dr. Thomas called out quickly, "Be careful with it! No one has touched that thing for four hundred years!"

Because the artifacts have been buried for so long, they might crumble when removed from the moist soil. It is important for the archaeologist to handle them gently and pack them securely.

Little clues and big finds brought equally triumphant cries from the excavators as they found piece after piece of the puzzle. Each crew member was able to make a real contribution to solving the mystery of St. Catherines; and every item, no matter how tiny or insignificant-looking, eventually brought answers about mission life on the island.

To the inexperienced bystander, getting excited about minuscule pieces of metal, bead, bone, and religious artifacts might have seemed ludicrous. But to archaeologists they are all important finds. As Dr. Thomas said, "It's not what you find but what you find out that counts." For instance, a broken piece of Italian pottery doesn't look like much. But finding any Italian or European pottery on the site showed the excavators that they were dealing with imported artifacts brought to North America by European explorers. It further confirmed that the site they were working in was of the mission period.

During the six years of actual excavation, some of the most valuable religious medals ever found in North America were unearthed on St. Catherines. Also found were thousands of beads, rare crosses, Indian remains, shrouds, glass bottles, finger rings, bell fragments, ceramics, and musket balls.

But as Dr. Thomas explained, "Little that is excavated is glitzy or of exhibition quality. We're looking for ecofacts—things like fish scales, animal bones, shells—which, when found in quantity, give real clues to the lifestyle, the dietary habits, and general health of the people of St. Catherines."

After each of the seventeen excavation trips, all of the discoveries were loaded onto the island boat and sent to the laboratories at the American Museum of Natural History in New York City or to specialists around the country for analysis and study. These scientists were able to shed further light on life on the island four hundred years ago. Their findings fueled David's continuing investigation.

7. *Research and Repair*

The research and repair teams back at the museum and at other locations are essentially explorers, too. These curators and conservators enhance and define the archaeological treasures unearthed by Dr. Thomas's field crews. For instance, a bag of soil is just a bag of soil until an expert studies its consistency and is able to tell what lived with and in it. Similarly, globs of encrusted material look no more distinct than bags of soil until conservators begin to remove the ancient coating and see for themselves what might be within. And often the museum artist, working carefully under a magnifying glass, discovers inscriptions and patterns on objects that are not easily seen with the naked eye.

These behind-the-scenes specialists work and report on everything they are sent. As one of the museum's conservators said, "When you commit yourself to archaeology, the objective of your work is to preserve the information found in the object. I might enjoy working on an ornate necklace rather than on a bunch of nails. But who's to say which artifact will contribute the most information to the project? Therefore, I feel everything I work on has equal importance."

45

For example, as she cleans an encrusted religious medal, she may uncover details and inscriptions. Frequently the information on such objects sheds a dramatic new light on the investigation. Consequently, everything the conservator does to or finds on an object is recorded and packed away with the item.

The most critical time for the archaeological artifacts is the first few weeks after they have been removed from the earth. They are coming from an environment where their equilibrium has been maintained for hundreds of years. Once in their above-ground environment, all the conditions are different, and they can be adversely affected by the change in temperature, light, and relative humidity. The conservator's first priority is to stabilize the objects. They will be valuable only if they remain intact for further study and analysis.

Some artifacts need very little work, while others are unrecognizable. Religious medals generally need a good scraping with a scalpel. If the medal has turned green, indicating corrosion, it must be dipped in a solution to prevent further damage. Other metallic objects may surface in relatively clean condition. In that case they need only be washed and polished. Working under a microscope, a conservator removes any dirt or deposits from the tiny crevices.

Ceramics, which are often found in pieces, must be cleaned and reassembled. Using a sand tray, the conservator stands up the various pieces and slowly glues them together. After the object has been rebuilt, the crevices and gaps are filled in with a special substance and sometimes painted in areas where the decoration has faded.

Conservators do not attempt to make an object look new. "After all," said one of the museum's curators, "we are not in the business of recreating or refurbishing an ancient handmade object. It should look real because it is real. Visitors come to see the artifact, not a replica. If something is beyond repair yet is important to an exhibition, we will have a copy made and indicate it as such."

Each new field trip to St. Catherines brought valuable insights into the life at the mission. Some of the most exciting information came when the mission church and cemetery were excavated and studied.

The mission on St. Catherines boasted one of the largest cemeteries that had ever been systematically excavated in North America. Buried under the floor of the chapel were the remains of hundreds of people. With them were found beads, ornate rosaries, crucifixes, and precious medals. While the religious artifacts were sent to conservators at the museum, the human bones were sent to a specialist in Illinois.

Before the bones left the site, though, they were cleaned and then painted with a plastic solution that preserves them indefinitely. Once in the specialist's laboratory, they were analyzed to determine the person's sex, cause of death, any disease he or she might have had, and the chemical composition of the bones.

Interesting information about diet emerged from these studies. It was determined that the Indians who lived under Spanish influence and adopted European agricultural methods developed more tooth decay and bone disease. Evidence from the bone studies seemed to indicate that it might have been more advantageous for the natives to continue hunting wild animals and eating only naturally grown food such as berries and nuts.

What archaeologists find out from the past may help future generations.

8. Sharing the Story

The site of the mission on St. Catherines Island has long since been found, and thousands of treasures have been amassed. But the archaeologists were not yet finished with the hunt. They now had to learn from the things they had found. "It is our job," said David Thomas, "to make sense out of other people's garbage. We have the finds, but now we have to ask ourselves what we have found out."

His work and the work of his staff went on until they were able to fit the pieces together and tell the whole story.

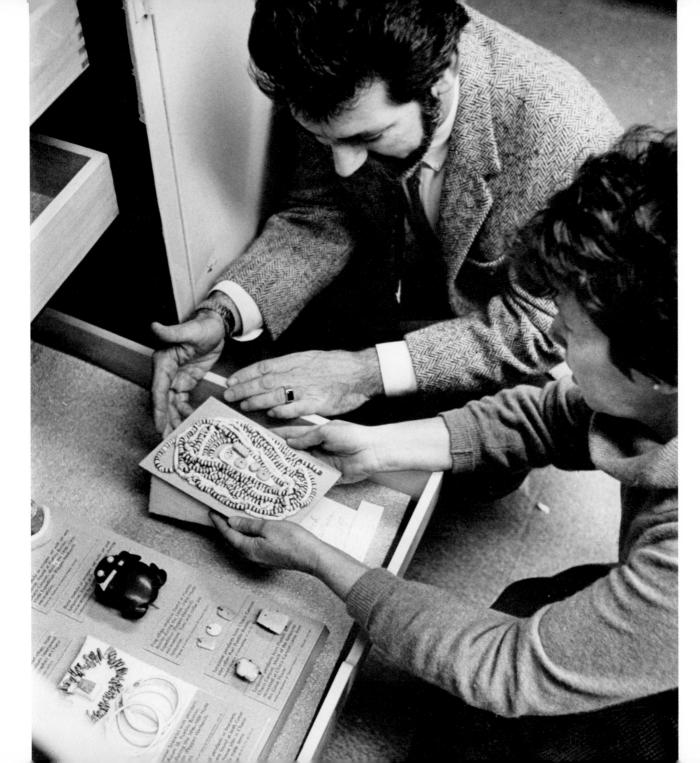

To start assembling the facts that might help to create a picture of life at the mission, David made frequent rounds to the different laboratories and departments where his data were still being analyzed and preserved. Research assistants were collating the thousands of pages of field notes, historical documentation, and charts. They were also busy writing detailed papers for the museum describing every aspect of the expedition.

Results from scientists such as mineralogists, soil specialists, geologists, bone experts, botanists, and historians kept pouring in as the months passed. Specialists in Spanish and Indian ceramics visited the museum to see what had been unearthed and to add their analysis. Experts in religious artifacts came, not only to contribute their knowledge but to view the precious pieces. David learned from them that many of the religious artifacts found on St. Catherines were unlike any others in the world!

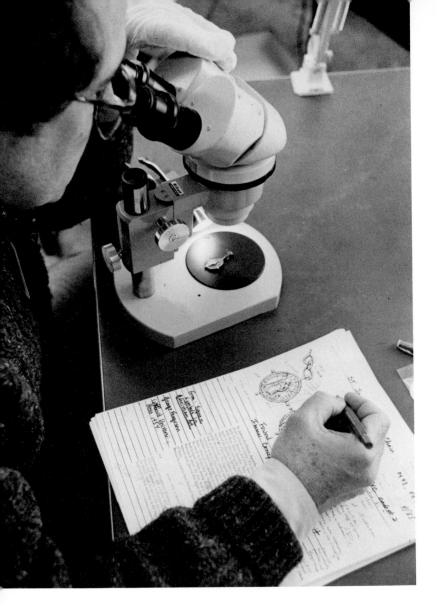

Restorers were hard at work as well, sorting out the thousands of shards of ceramics in hopes of being able to piece together some of them. They also attempted to define and catalog them by looking carefully at the designs and trying to identify their style and period.

The artifacts that were not being studied or conserved at the moment were kept in storage rooms and drawers. Cataloguers had attached a written description to every object in the collection, and sometimes an artist's drawing or photograph as well. They had also included a form that told the origin of the piece, when and where it was found, how it came to the museum, and the date of receipt. All these details helped David place each object in the overall array of objects.

And from the mass of facts that were coming in, he was now able to begin fitting the pieces together. By discovering a series of burned posts on the mission floor, for example, Dr. Thomas was able to confirm the eyewitness accounts in historical journals that, indeed, the mission had been burned to the ground at least once. The friars and the Guales must have lived in constant danger of attack from the north by the British and French who were also trying to gain a foothold in North America at the time.

He learned that the Guales were a sophisticated nation and therefore one the Spanish would have needed to befriend. It became clearer and clearer as evidence came in that the chief had in fact lived on St. Catherines, thus making it one of the more significant settlements in the Southeast for European explorers.

With the thorough reports of the geologists, mineralogists, bone experts, and others, David Thomas also began to see clearly the daily lifestyle of the friars and the Indians. He could make informed surmises about their agricultural methods, food sources, religious rituals, burial practices, housing arangements, and settlement patterns.

This is the stuff that exhibits are made of. With a real story of a people and a time falling into place, it was now possible to share this information with the public. After all, the driving force behind most museums is to teach; and by displaying a collection exhibitors hope to enhance the public's understanding and appreciation of the past, to bring people closer to times, places, and societies they have never known.

"Well, gentlemen," Dr. Thomas says to the journalists, "I think I've answered your questions . . . yes? Now you know how we found the lost mission and can see how these artifacts got here. Pretty amazing, isn't it?"

"Where do you go next?" another reporter inquires.

"Well, I haven't finished with St. Catherines yet. We've only uncovered the mission. I'm gratified that this exploration is able to fill a void in early American history. But all those Guale structures in the surrounding area surely have their own stories to tell. And then, of course, I never know who will be on the other end of the phone when I pick it up. We're only beginning to scratch the earth's surface, you know."

And with that, David nods goodbye and heads home.

How Did These Things Get Here?

There are hundreds of explorer-scientists like David Thomas roaming the world, uncovering mysteries of what the earth and its people hold. They are venturesome spirits, but also dedicated, knowledgeable, precise, and ready to devote a lifetime to answering elusive questions and learning about various cultures.

There are basically two ways to study societies: to find existing groups of people while they are still alive and observe them firsthand, or to dig up ancient cultures and attempt to understand these people from the things they left behind.

The scientists who study living people are called anthropologists. They spend years, sometimes a lifetime, observing the appearance, customs, technologies, and diet of these groups. Those scientists whose subjects are dead are called archaeologists. They, too, ask the same questions, but their task is obviously more difficult. Digging deep into the earth's surface, they excavate buildings, artifacts, and human and animal remains; after careful analysis they try to determine how the people once lived.

Whichever approach they take, these adventurous detectives study the evolution of human beings by posing thousands of questions. As they collect answers, a story begins to emerge.

The storage rooms of museums become the home for their findings. The collections are available to historians and researchers, and eventually some of these collections become exhibits. Either way the findings remain valuable to those who seek to uncover the secrets of human cultures, past and present.

From Map to Museum is the story of how one collection was amassed. To follow the process from the very beginning, we have looked beyond the glass display cases to the museum storage rooms and the offices of the curators. We have traveled beyond the city streets upon which the museum sits to a tropical island where one modern-day explorer has been working for over fifteen years to uncover a lost mission and the culture of an extinct group of Indians.

We chose Dr. Thomas because he is well known in his field and affiliated with one of the largest natural history museums in the world. Moreover, he is pioneering new methods for seeking out and finding archaeological sites, utilizing space-age technology in the search. Finally, his story traces the process by which many artifacts and newly uncovered truths make their way into museums.

Perhaps the next time you visit a museum you will take with you an insider's knowledge of how the artifacts got there and how their story came to light.

Glossary

anthropology—the study of humankind as manifested in societies and customs

archaeology—the study of ancient peoples by scientific excavation of physical remains

artifact—any object used or manufactured by humans, such as ceramic pots, potshards, weapons, and jewels

botanist—a scientist who studies plants

cataloguer—a person who systematically records items and arranges them in such a way that they can be easily found

conservator—a person specially trained to stabilize, repair, and restore artifacts

corrosion—the process whereby a substance has been worn away by chemical reaction and partially destroyed

curator—a person in charge of museum and other collections

data—relevant observations made on objects, serving as a basis for study

daub—the wall surface or the material from a wall surface, such as hardened mud and straw

dig—another name for an archaeological excavation

ecofacts—the nonartificial remains found in an archaeological site, such as seeds, bones, and plant pollen

excavation—the act of methodically clearing an area and searching through the soil for structures and artifacts inhabited and used by persons long ago

feature—a find at an excavation site, such as a post, pillar, or any large, stationary object that is best left in place during the excavation. These finds are studied on location; pictures are drawn and photographs are taken of them without their removal from the site

field notes—all data and drawings recorded by crew members at the excavation site

field study—the research conducted at an excavation site or the nearby environment

field team—people who work at an excavation site

geologist—a person who studies soil, rocks, and the earth's crust and strata

grid—a system of numbered squares printed on a map, forming the basis for references to a particular place

magnetometer—a machine that monitors the magnetic character of the earth and indicates the presence of archaeological materials

mineralogist—a scientist who studies natural inorganic substances in the earth

mound—an elevation of earth or stones, often earth heaped over a grave

power auger—a tool with a screw at the tip used for boring into the earth

project artist—the person responsible for all graphics, photography, and drawings made of an archaeological site and the artifacts found there

quad—an arbitrary grid designation that measures 100 meters to a side

restoration—the process of bringing artifacts back to their original or near-original state by rebuilding and repairing them

screener—a person who looks through sifted soil and picks out small pieces of seed, bone, pottery, and so on from various units in an archaeological site

shards—broken piece of earthenware found in and around excavation sites

site—the ground in which archaeological material is found

soil resistivity—a technique used by archaeologists to determine the presence of subsurface features

stabilize—to firmly fix or establish an object or artifact so that it does not change its status or disintegrate further

surface site—an archaeological site that is evident only from surface remains and does not extend below the ground

test pits—small, systematically excavated archaeological tests

unit—the square area inside the confines of a marked-off excavation site where one person works and is responsible for all the data found there

Index

Photographs and maps are in *italics*.